AF254859

I Decorated My Heart for Christmas

Written by Jan Asleson
Illustrated/Design Layout by Jan Asleson

ISBN 9780578322995

Library of Congress Control Number 2021922813

Printed in the United States of America by Ingram Spark/Lightning Source

Published by Spirit Wings Designs 2021
daslpacker55@yahoo..com

Visit me at www.spiritwings designs.com

I DECORATED MY HEART FOR CHRISTMAS

CREATED BY

JAN ASLESON

This beautifully illustrated Christmas book contains a powerful message. Too often we focus on the trappings of Christmas - the decorations, the food and the presents and forget about Jesus, the reason we celebrate. For those of us who can't physically do what we once did, this book by my sister and friend is a welcome reminder to let Christ decorate our hearts!

Vaneetha Risner, author of *Walking Through Fire: A Memoir of Loss and Redemption*

Jan's heartfelt prose and beautiful illustrations are a reminder that our real Christmas celebration is a matter of the heart - that true spiritual place where the Child-turned-King rules and reigns.

James Thornber, author of *Better with Every Breath: The Journey From Loss to Living Again* and *Taking Off My Comfortable Clothes: Removing Religion to Find Relationship*

This book is dedicated to:

Wonderful Counselor
Mighty God
Everlasting Father
Prince of Peace

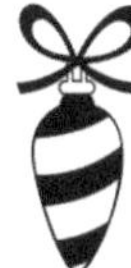

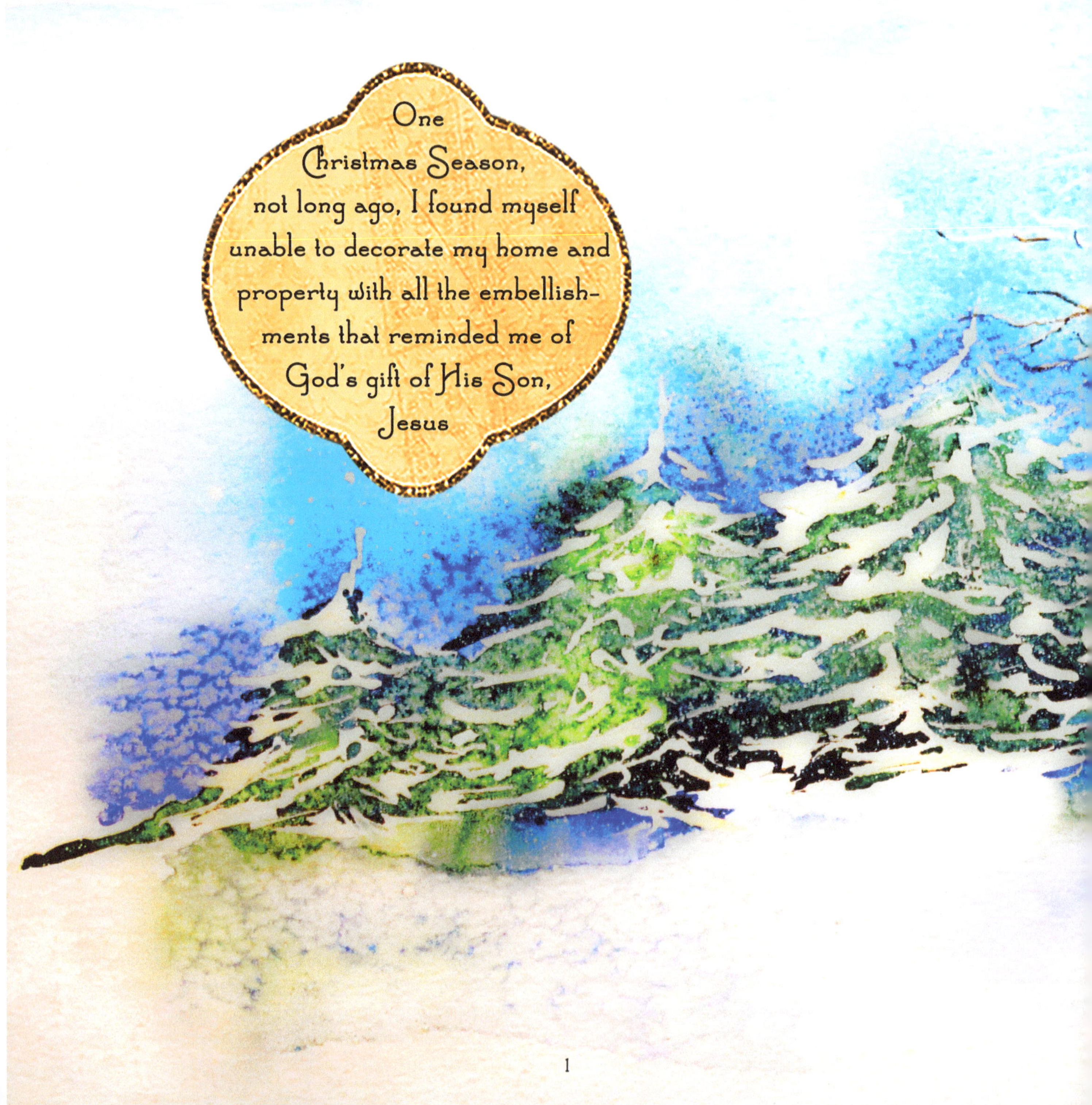

One
Christmas Season,
not long ago, I found myself
unable to decorate my home and
property with all the embellish-
ments that reminded me of
God's gift of His Son,
Jesus

1

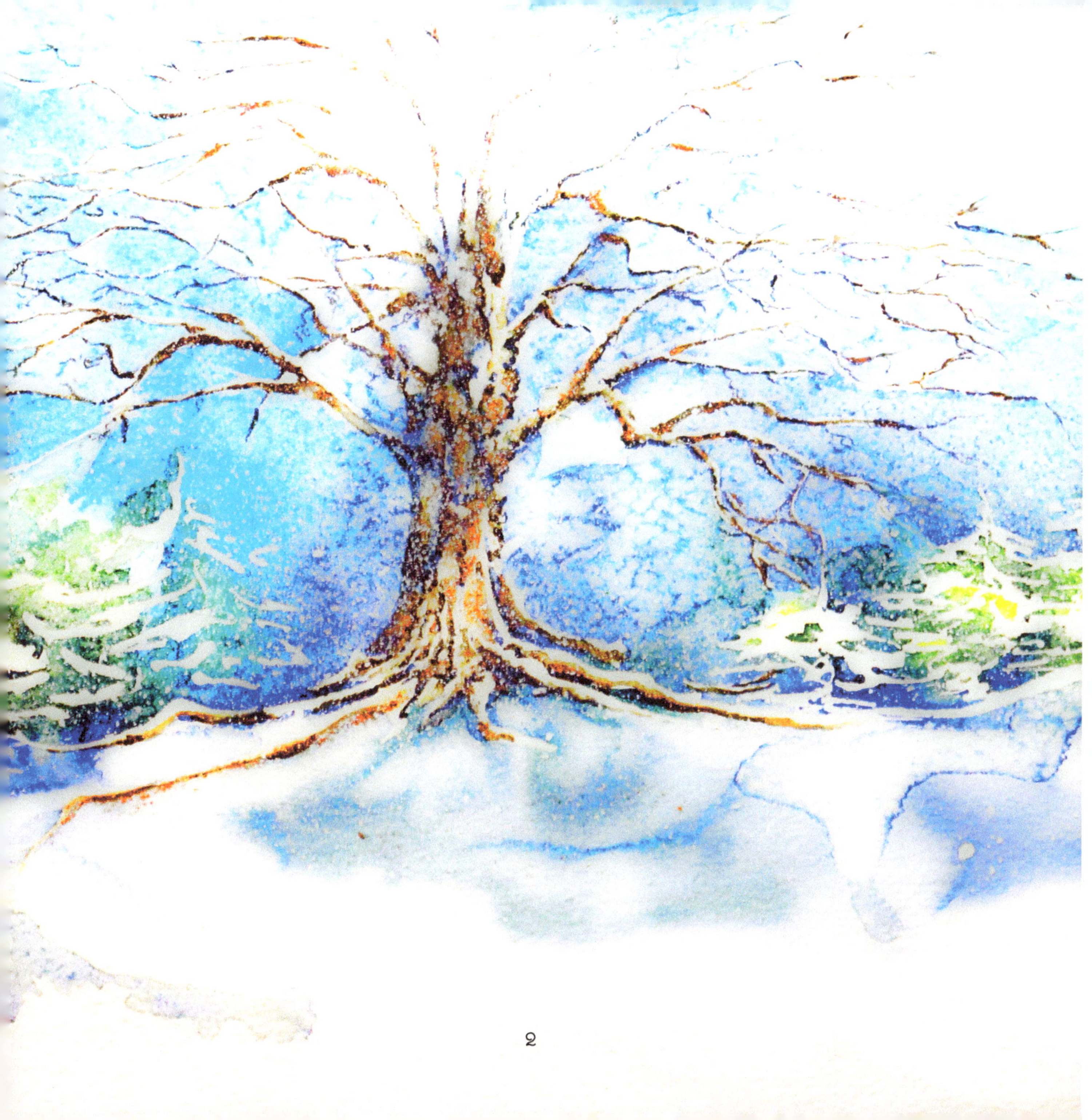

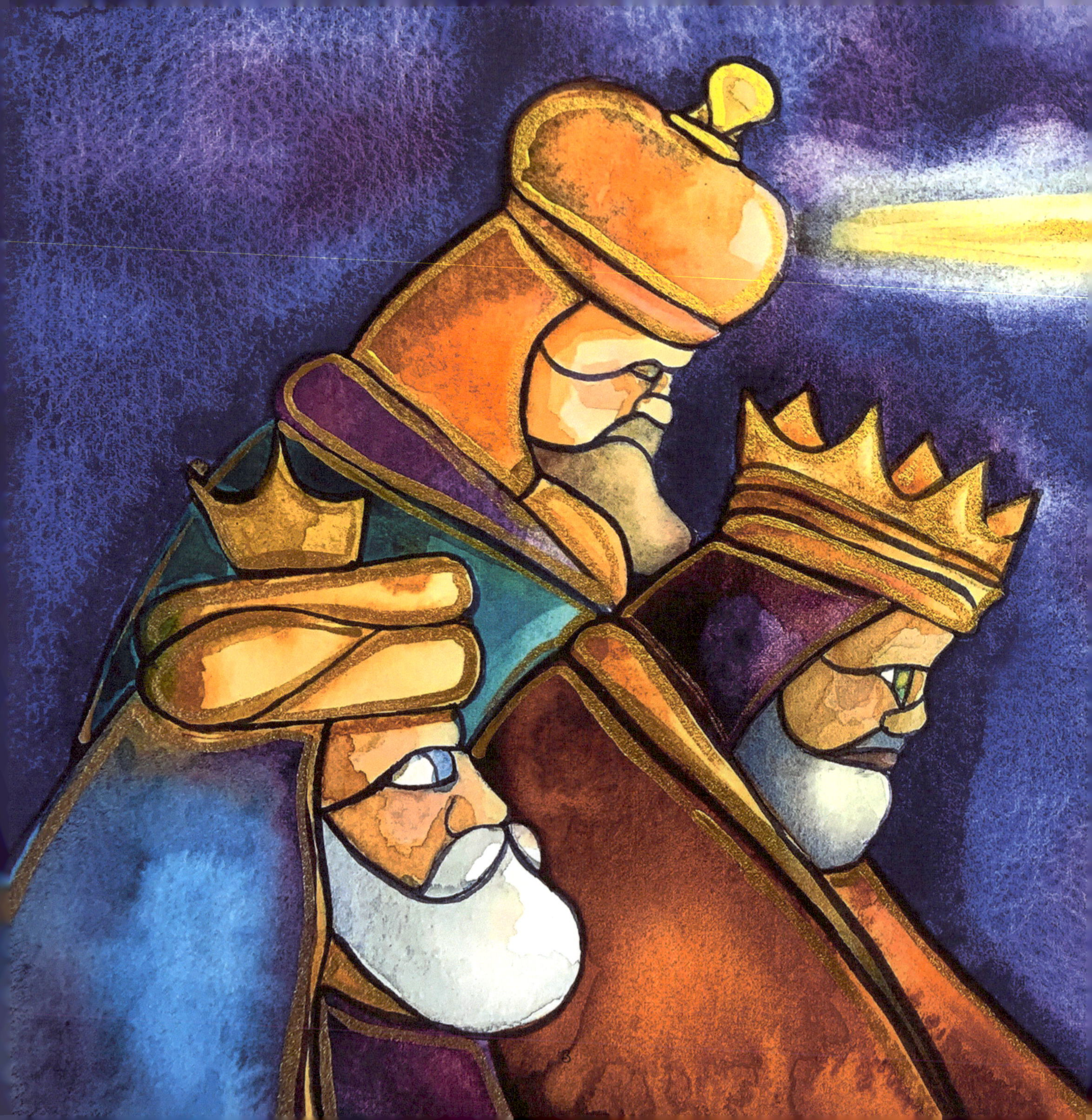

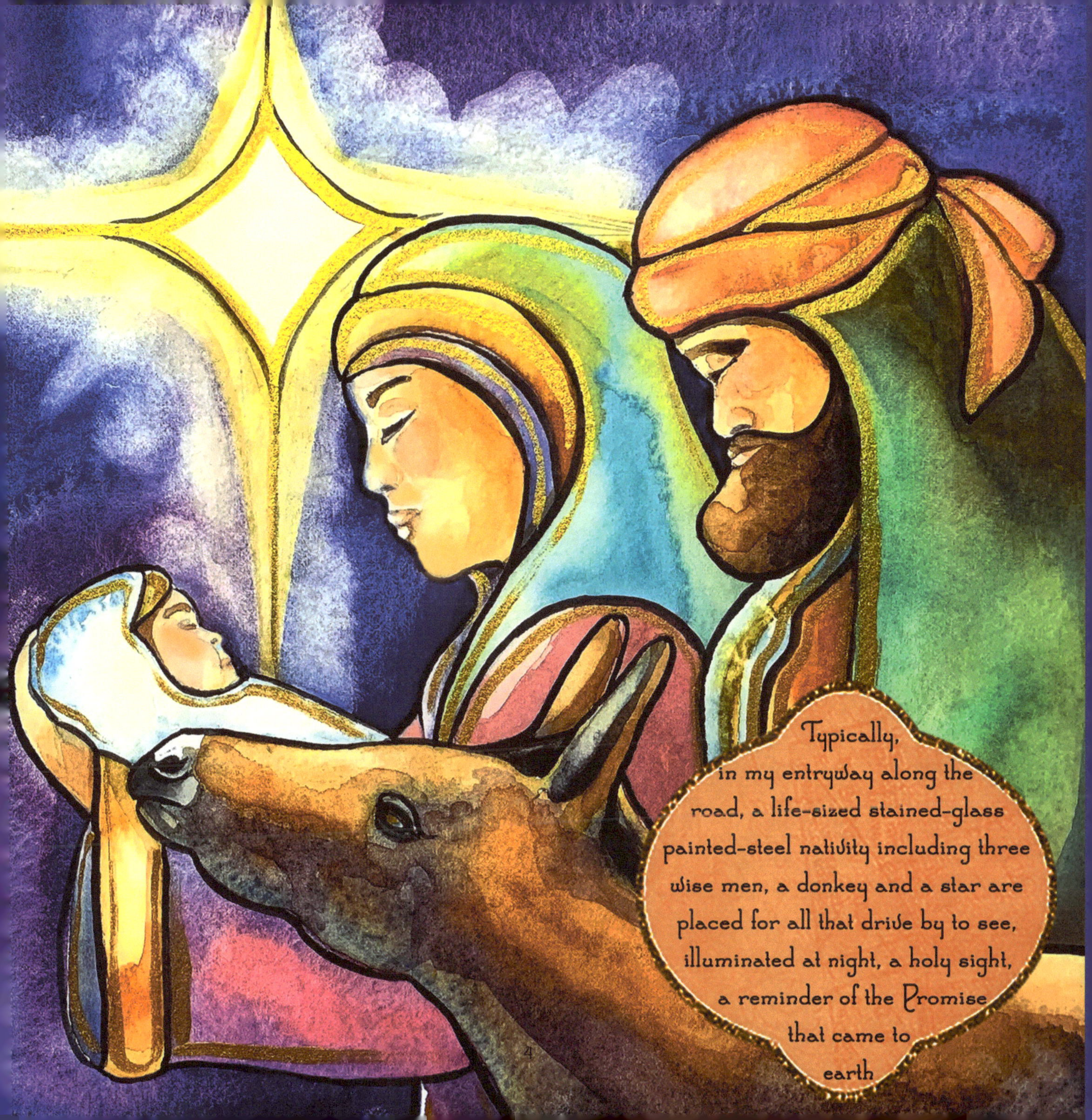
Typically,
in my entryway along the
road, a life-sized stained-glass
painted-steel nativity including three
wise men, a donkey and a star are
placed for all that drive by to see,
illuminated at night, a holy sight,
a reminder of the Promise
that came to
earth

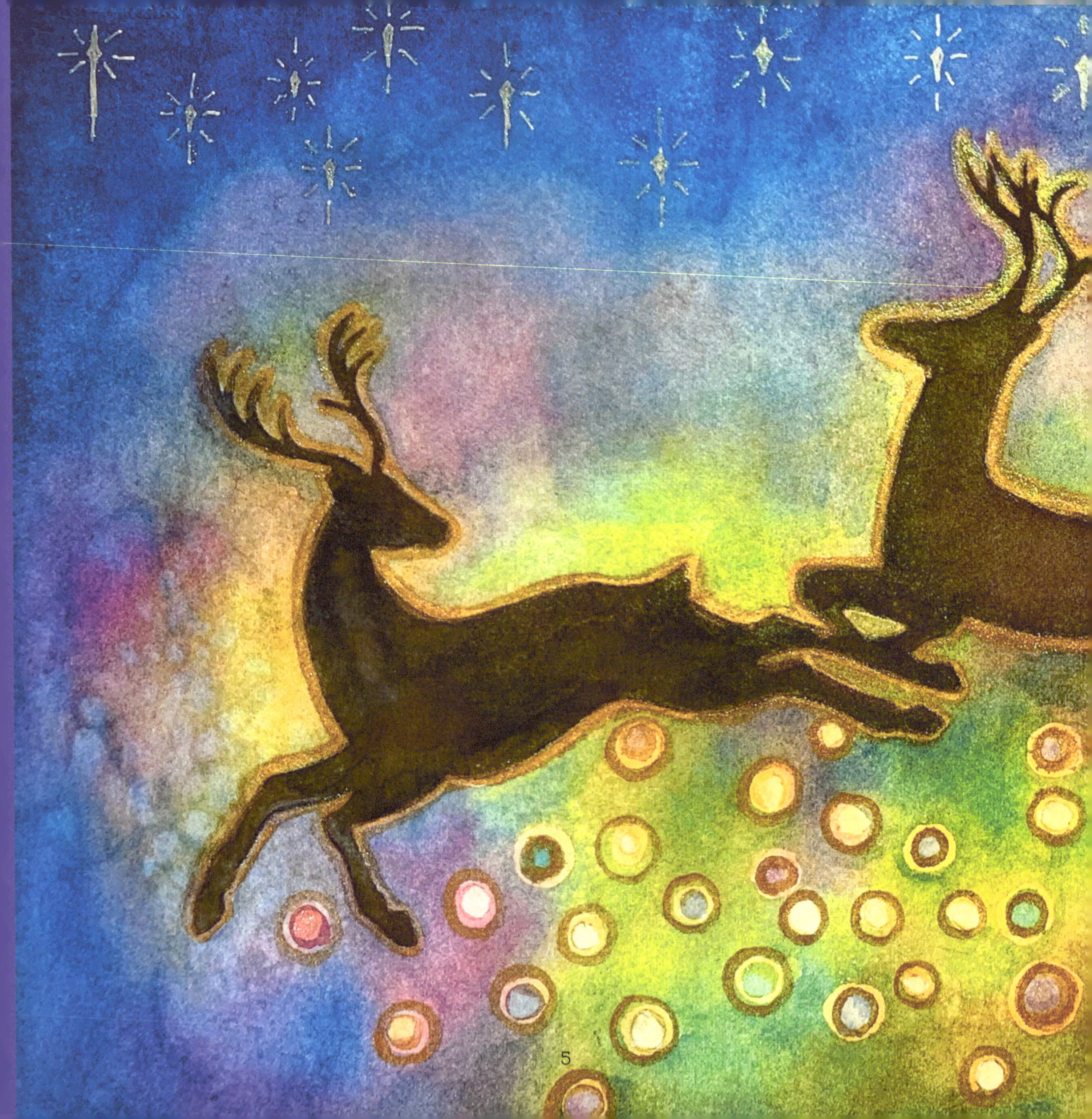

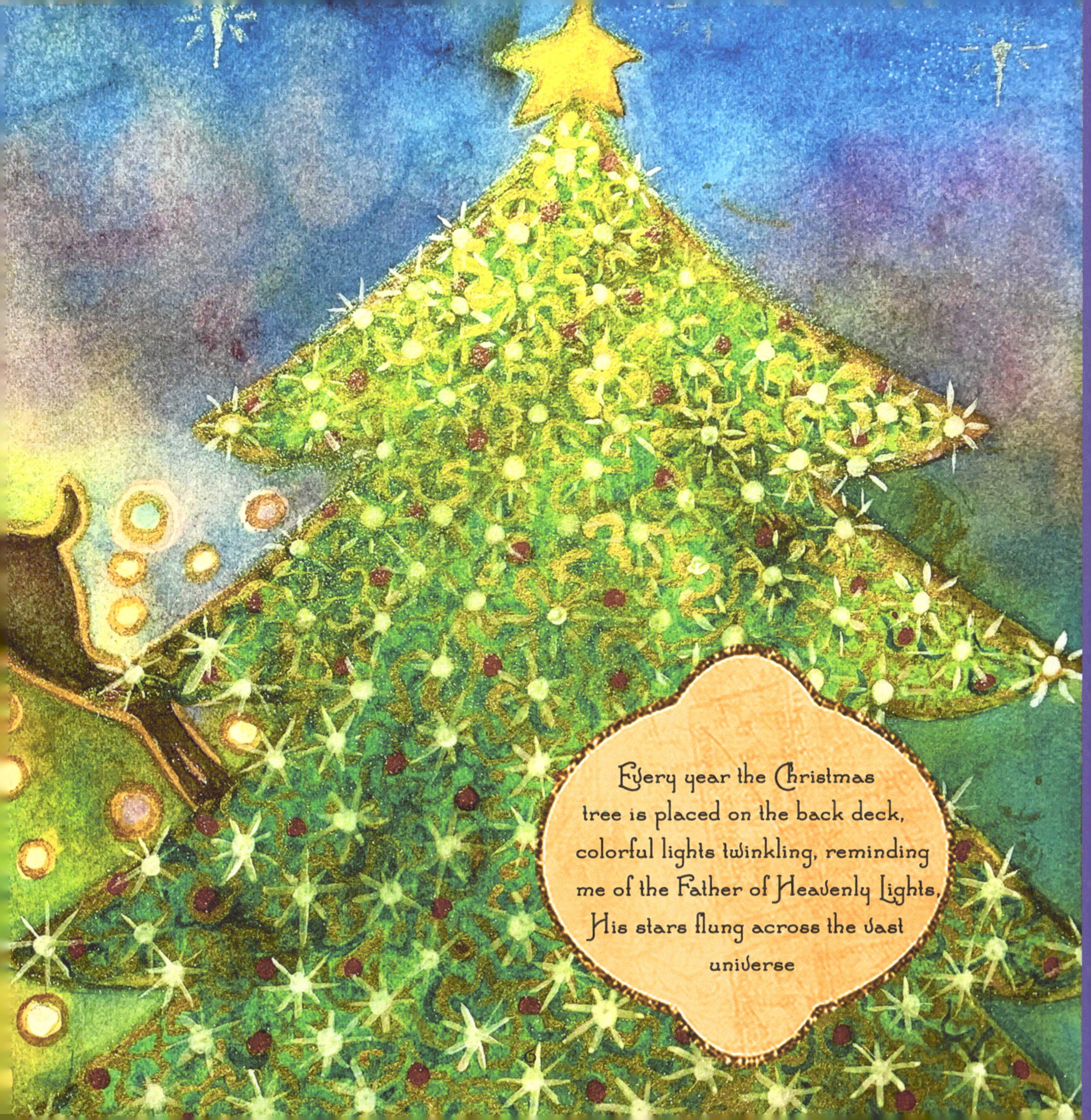

Every year the Christmas
tree is placed on the back deck,
colorful lights twinkling, reminding
me of the Father of Heavenly Lights,
His stars flung across the vast
universe

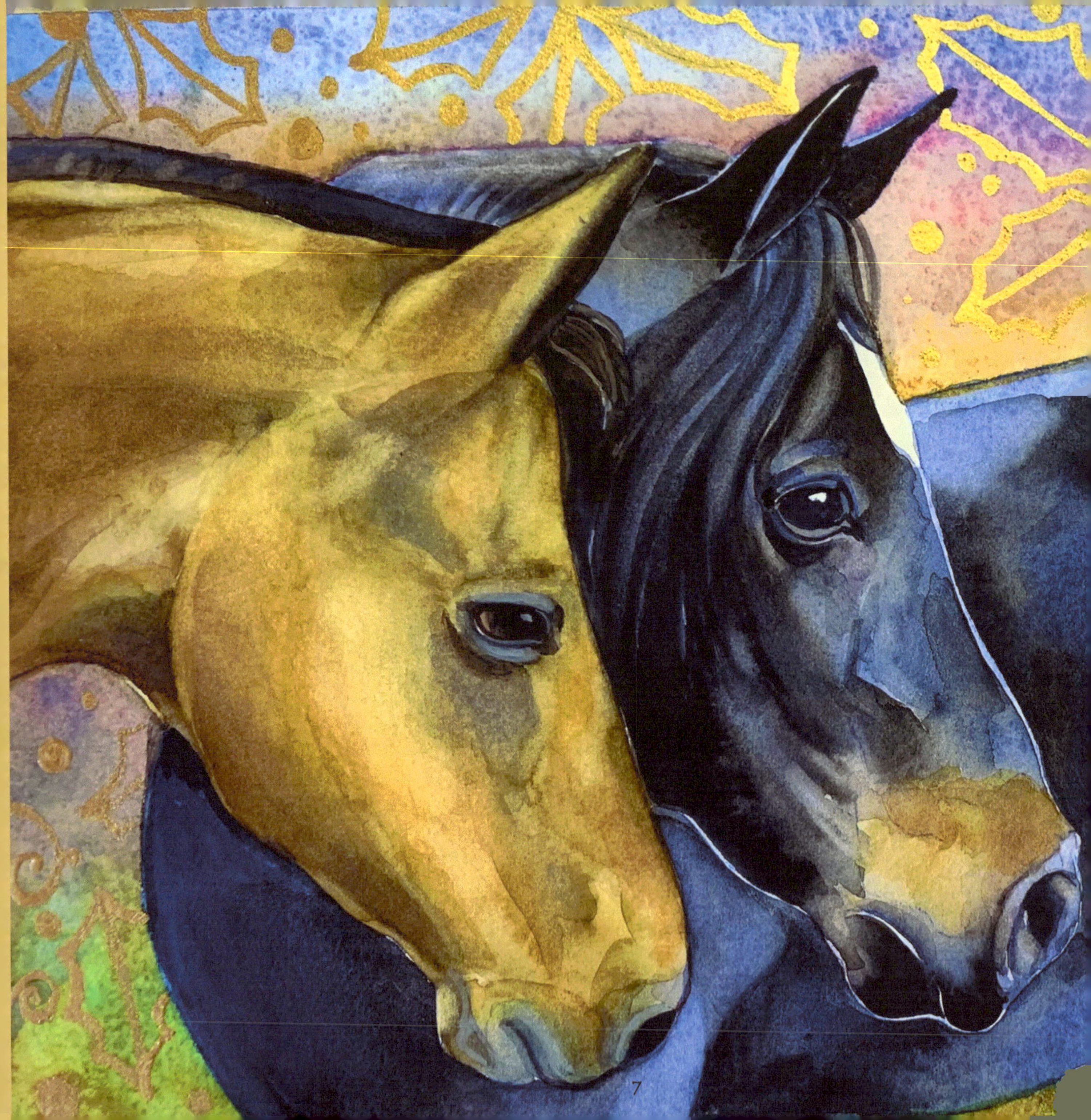

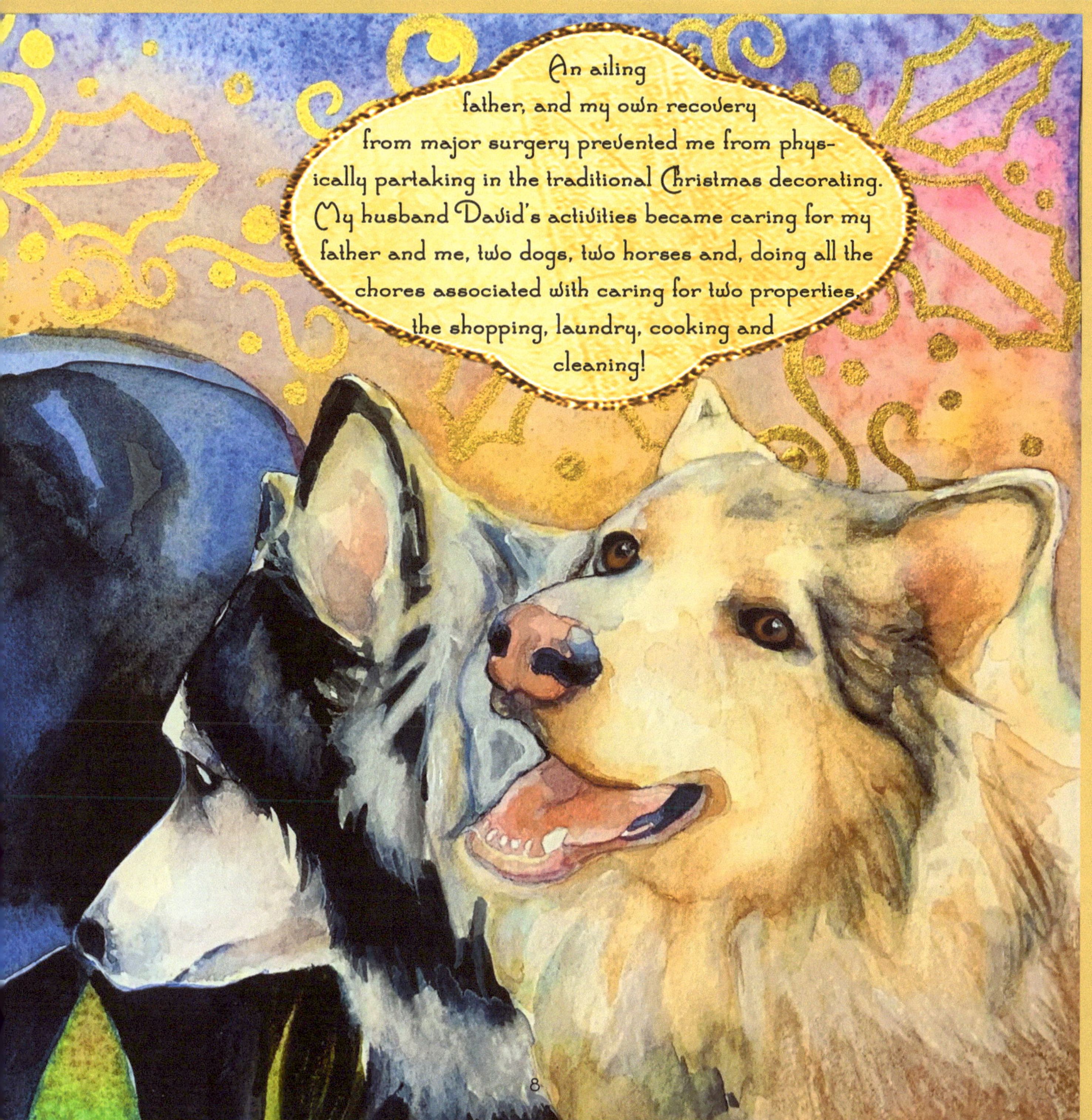

An ailing father, and my own recovery from major surgery prevented me from physically partaking in the traditional Christmas decorating. My husband David's activities became caring for my father and me, two dogs, two horses and, doing all the chores associated with caring for two properties, the shopping, laundry, cooking and cleaning!

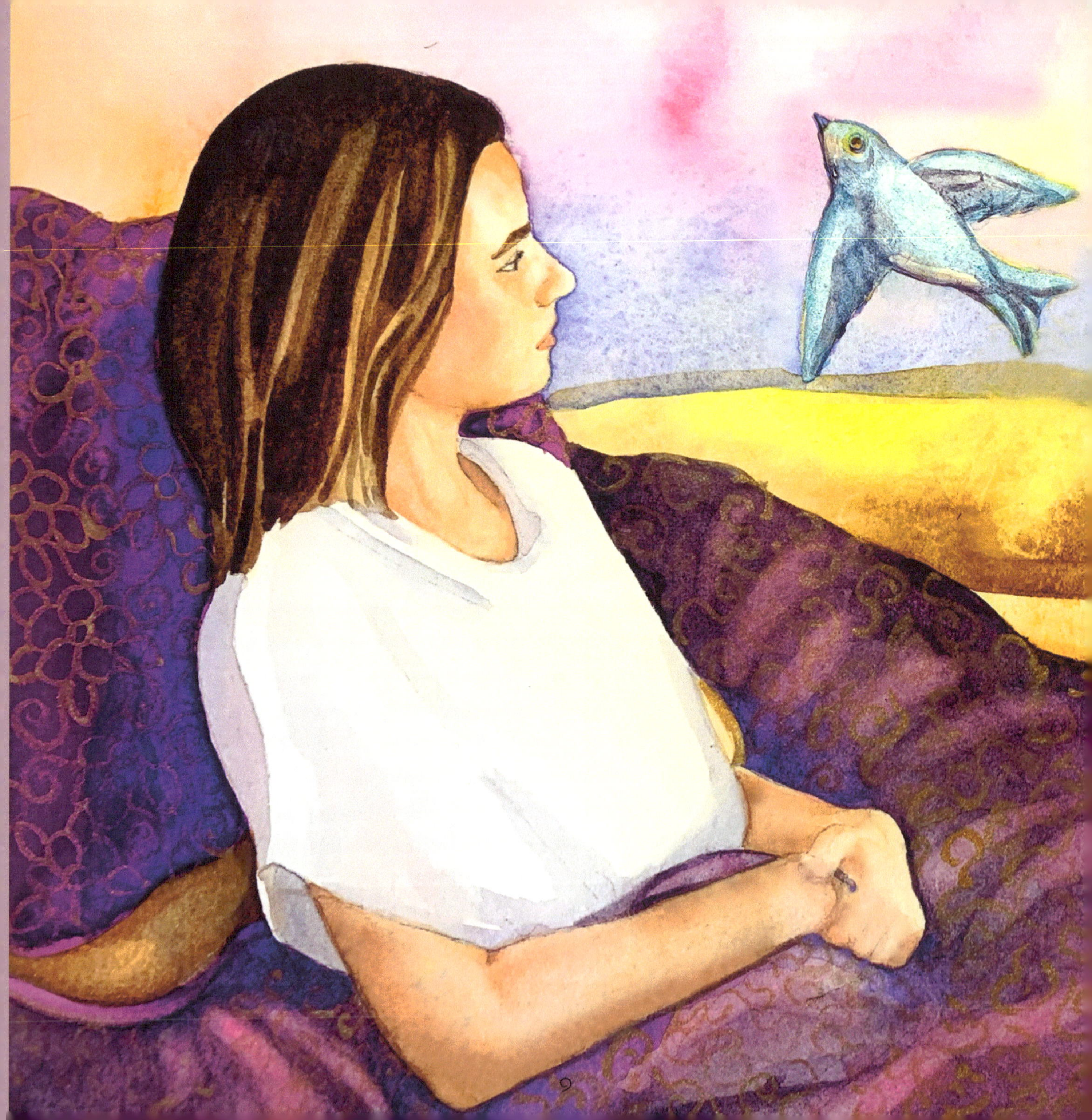

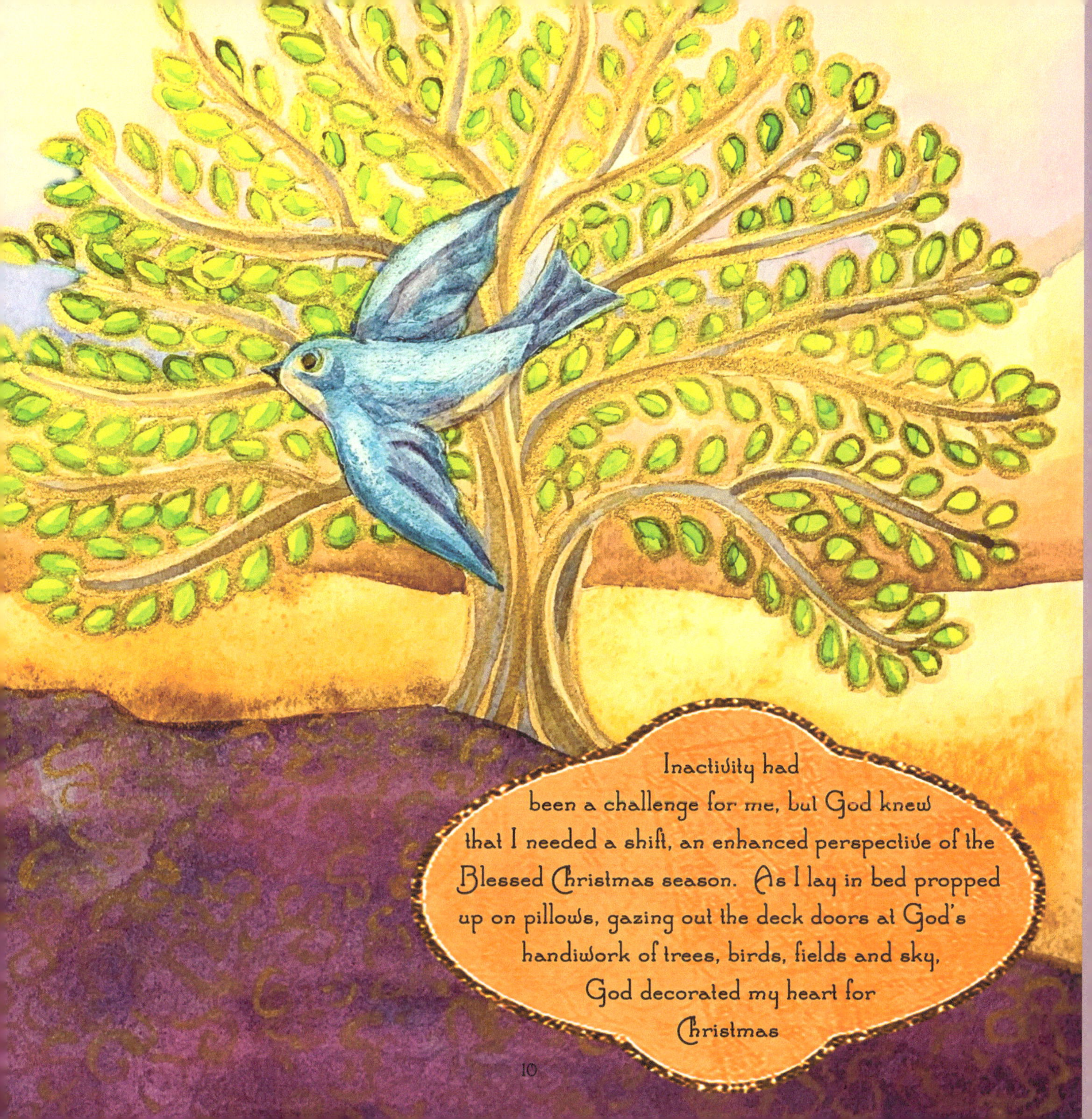

Inactivity had
been a challenge for me, but God knew
that I needed a shift, an enhanced perspective of the
Blessed Christmas season. As I lay in bed propped
up on pillows, gazing out the deck doors at God's
handiwork of trees, birds, fields and sky,
God decorated my heart for
Christmas

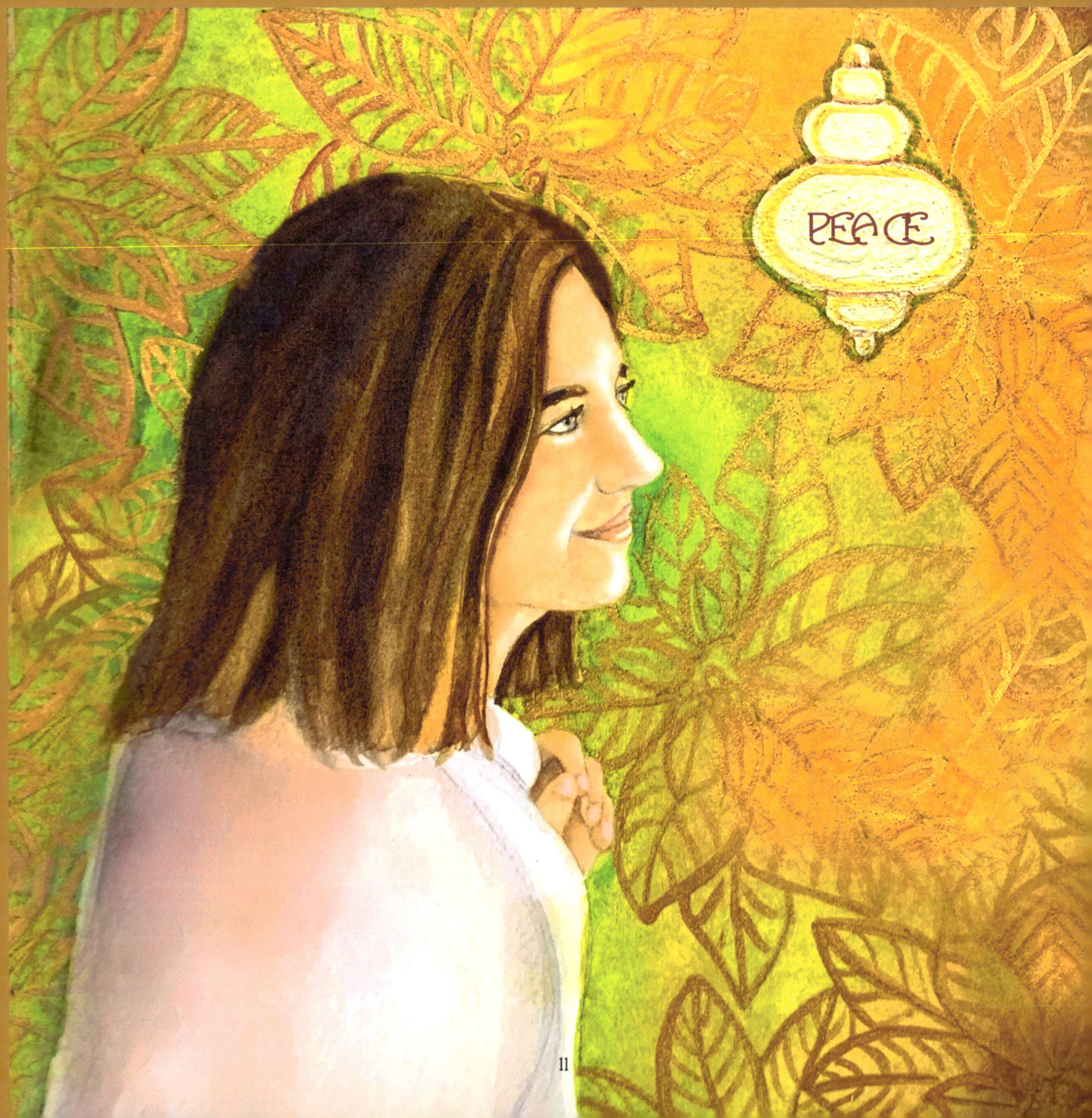

PEACE

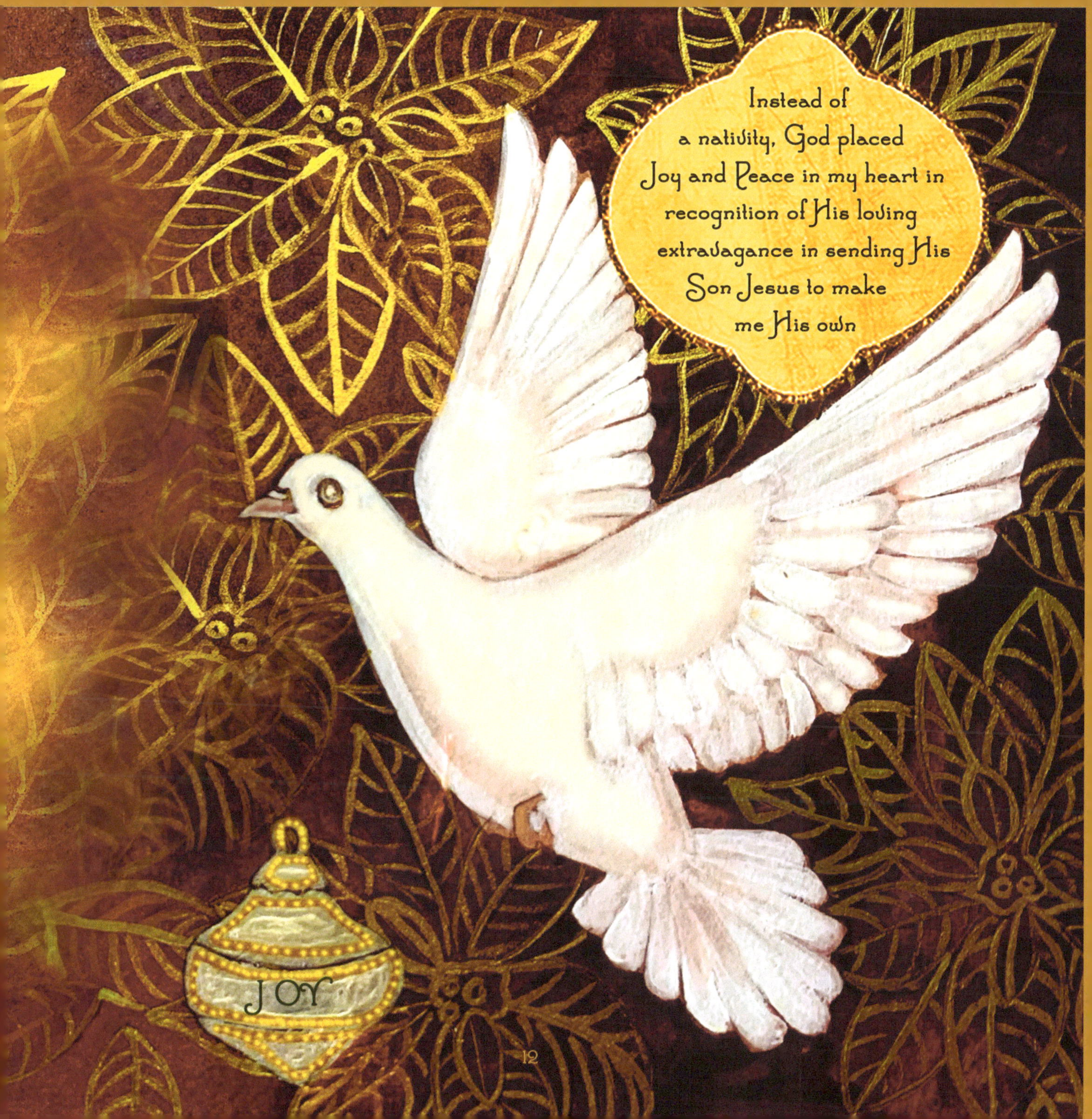

Instead of
a nativity, God placed
Joy and Peace in my heart in
recognition of His loving
extravagance in sending His
Son Jesus to make
me His own
JOY

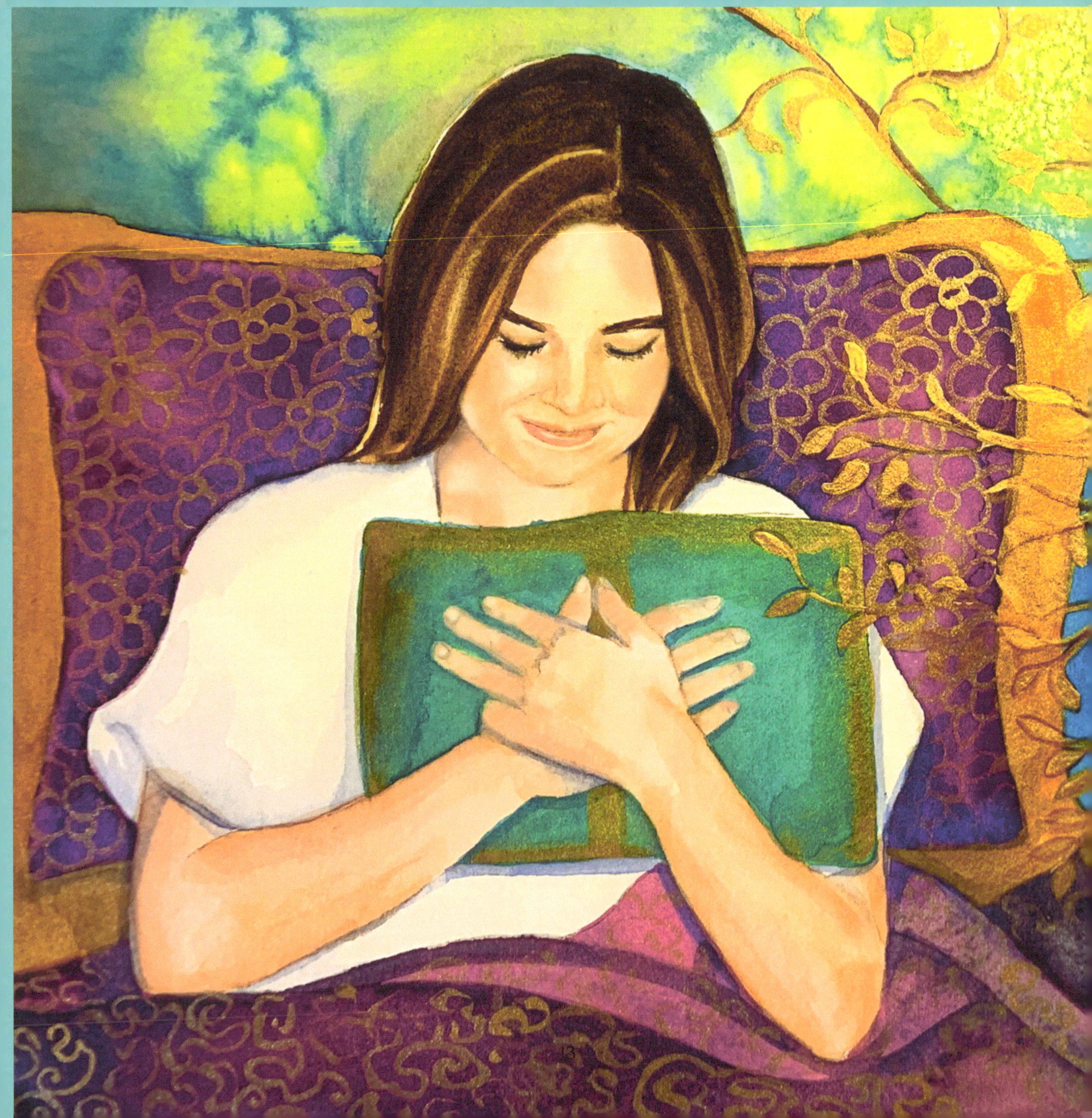

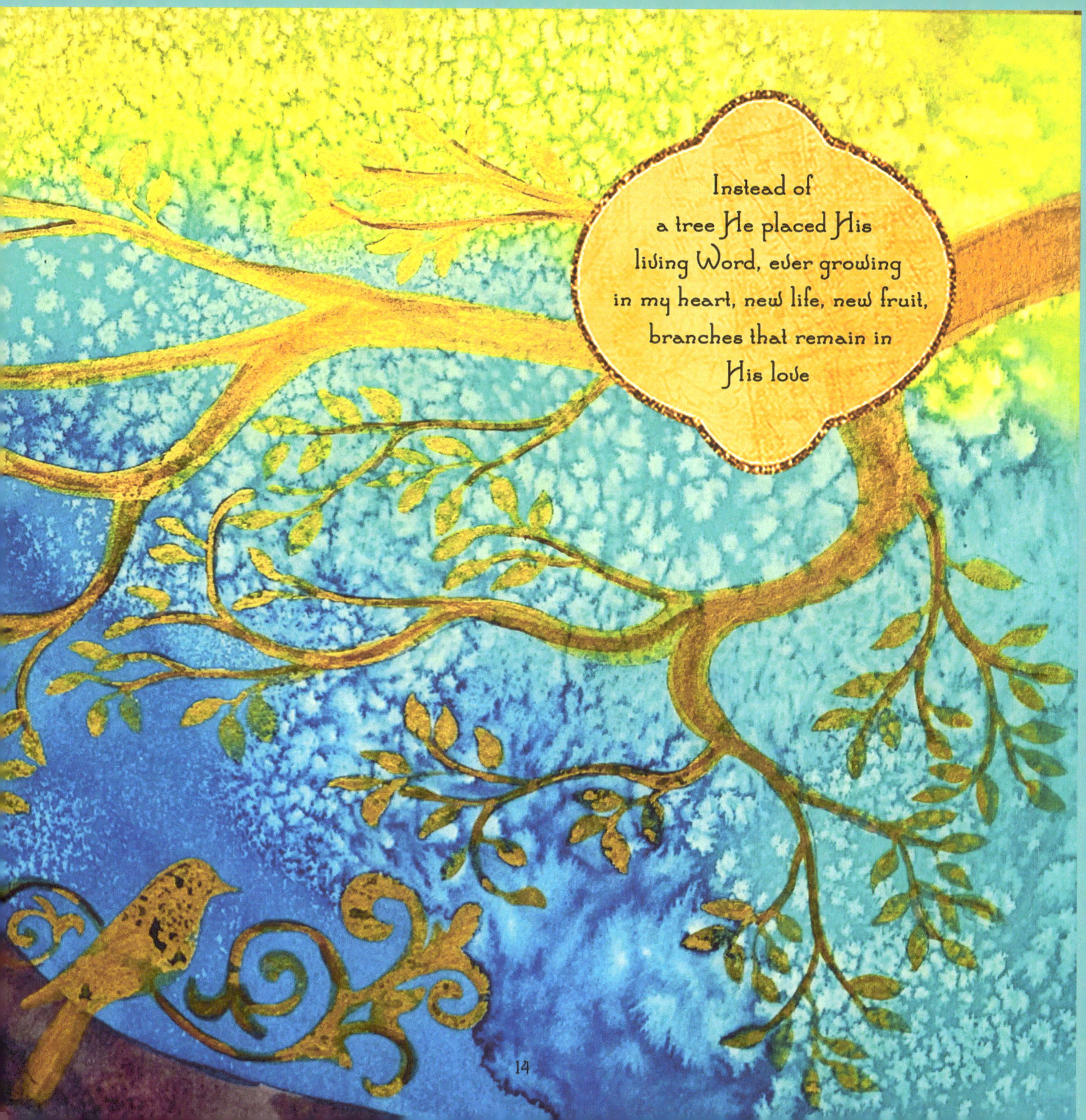

Instead of
a tree He placed His
living Word, ever growing
in my heart, new life, new fruit,
branches that remain in
His love

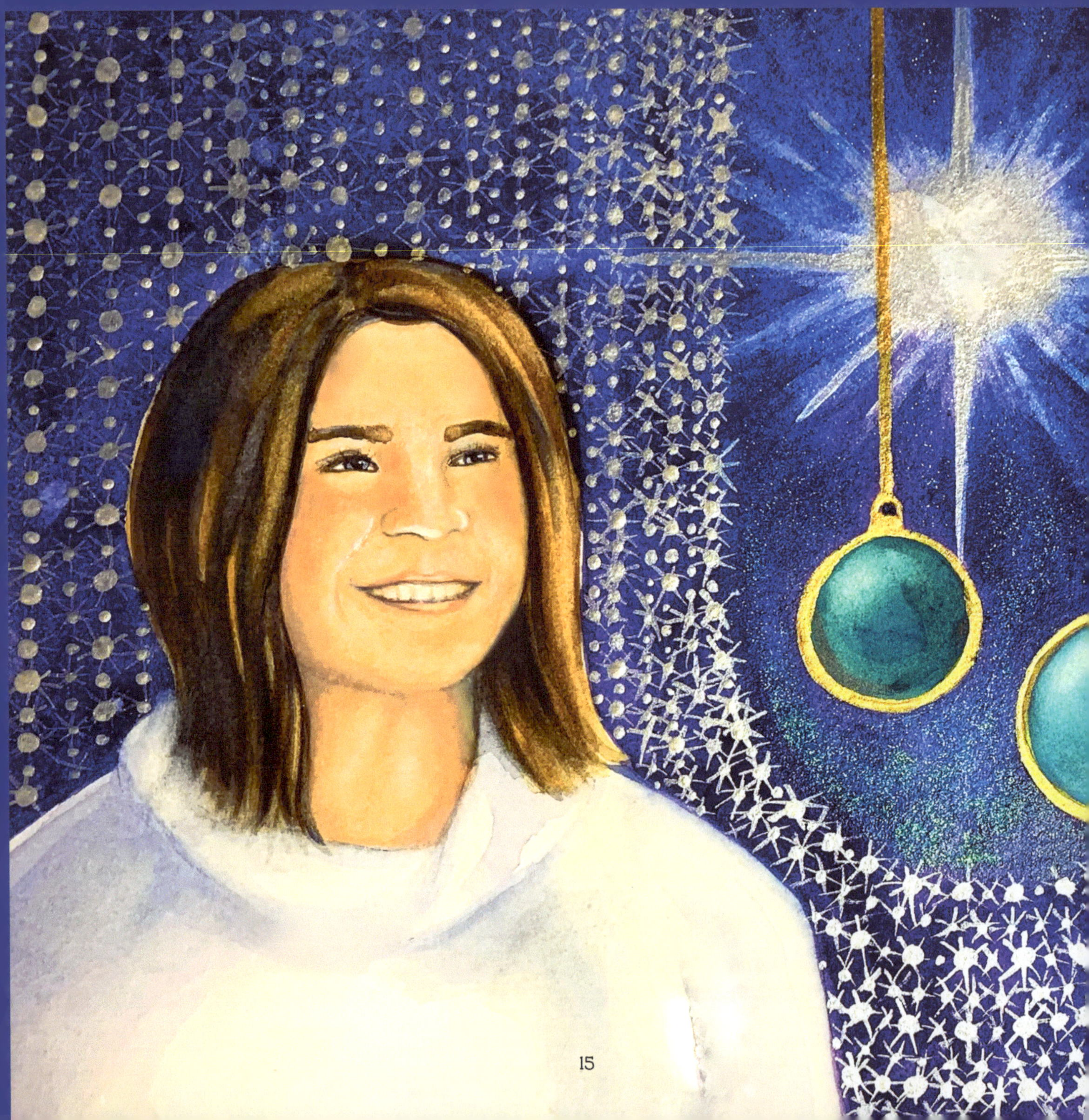

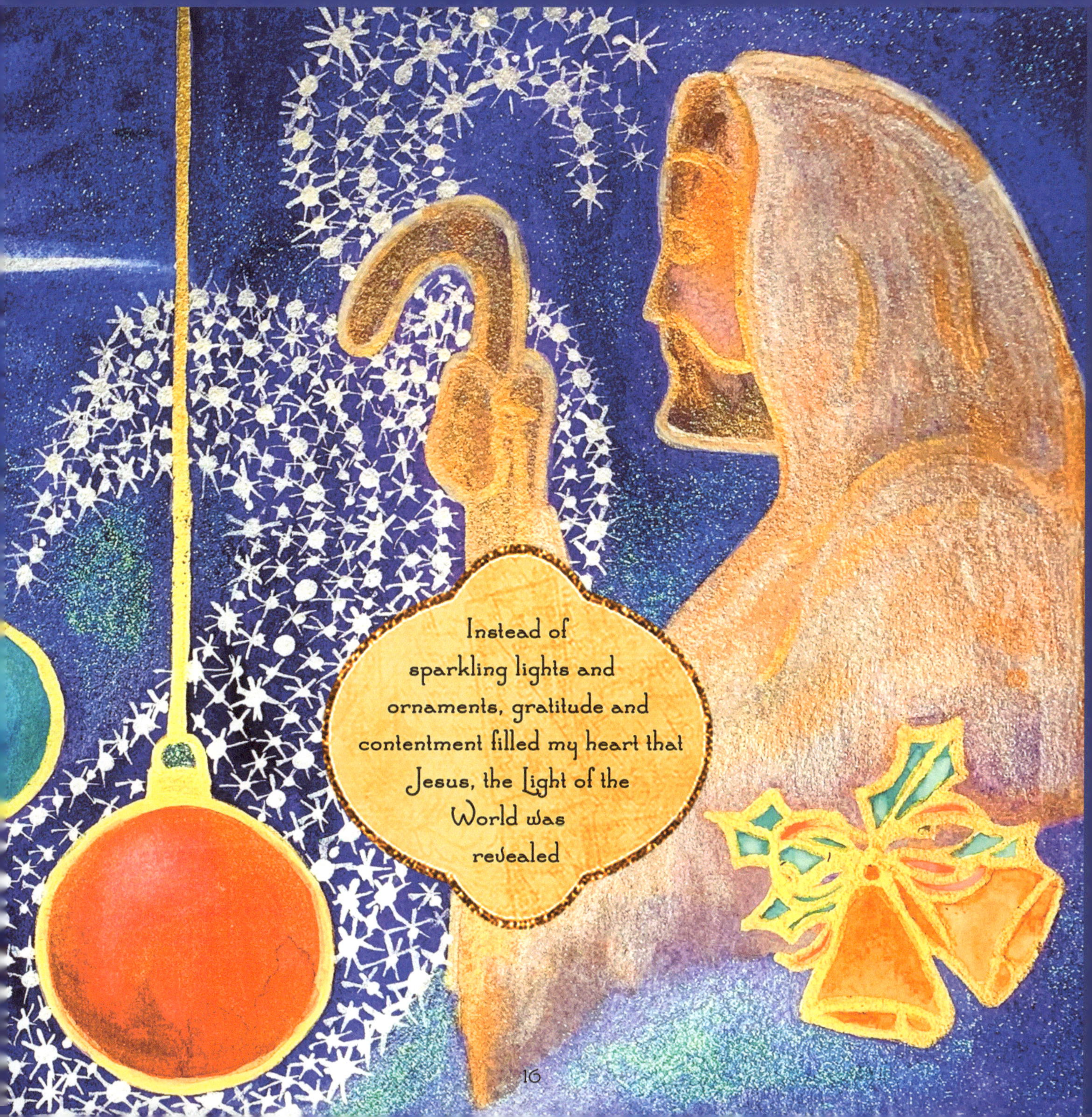

Instead of
sparkling lights and
ornaments, gratitude and
contentment filled my heart that
Jesus, the Light of the
World was
revealed

16

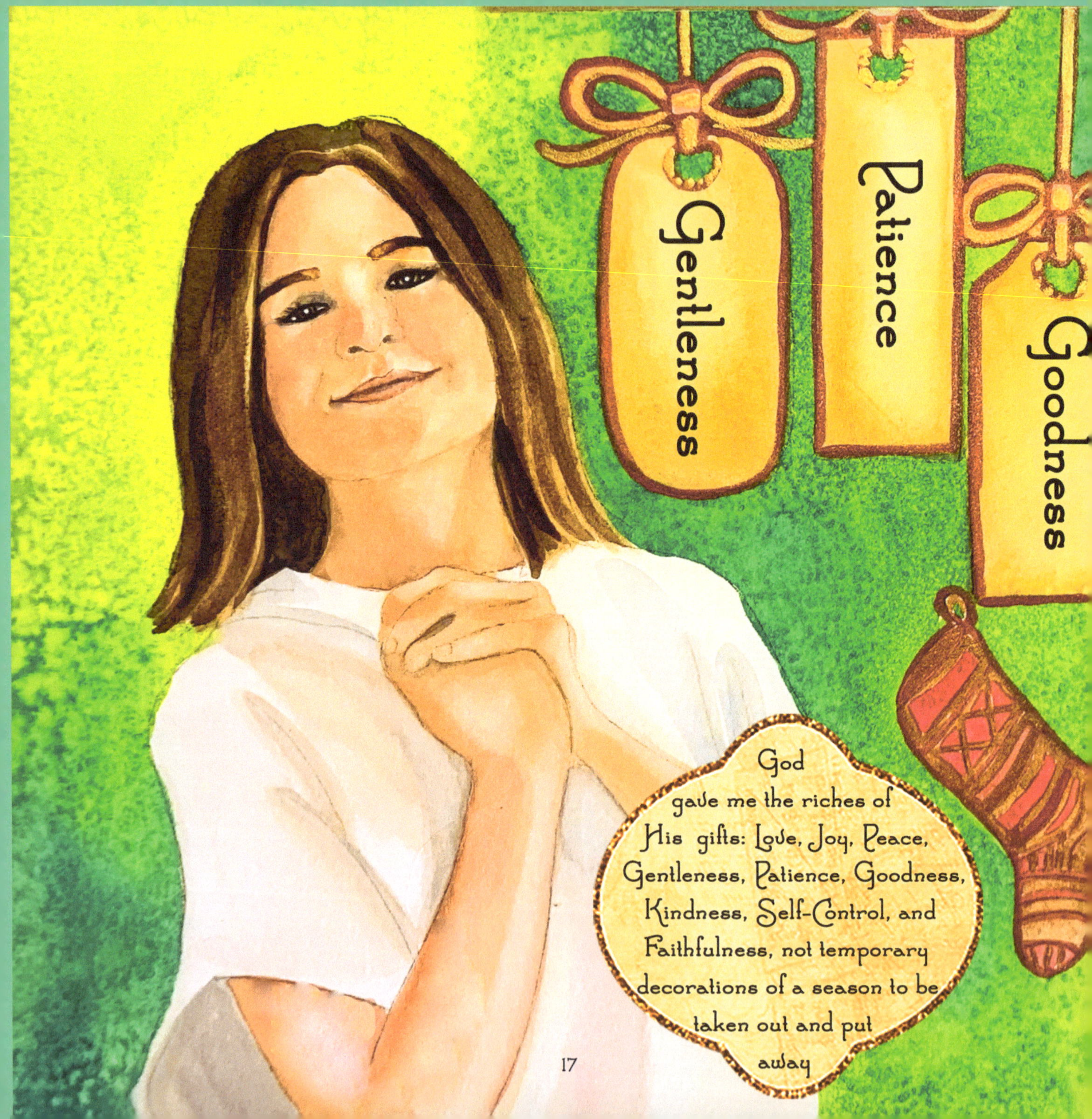

Gentleness
Patience
Goodness
God gave me the riches of His gifts: Love, Joy, Peace, Gentleness, Patience, Goodness, Kindness, Self-Control, and Faithfulness, not temporary decorations of a season to be taken out and put away
17

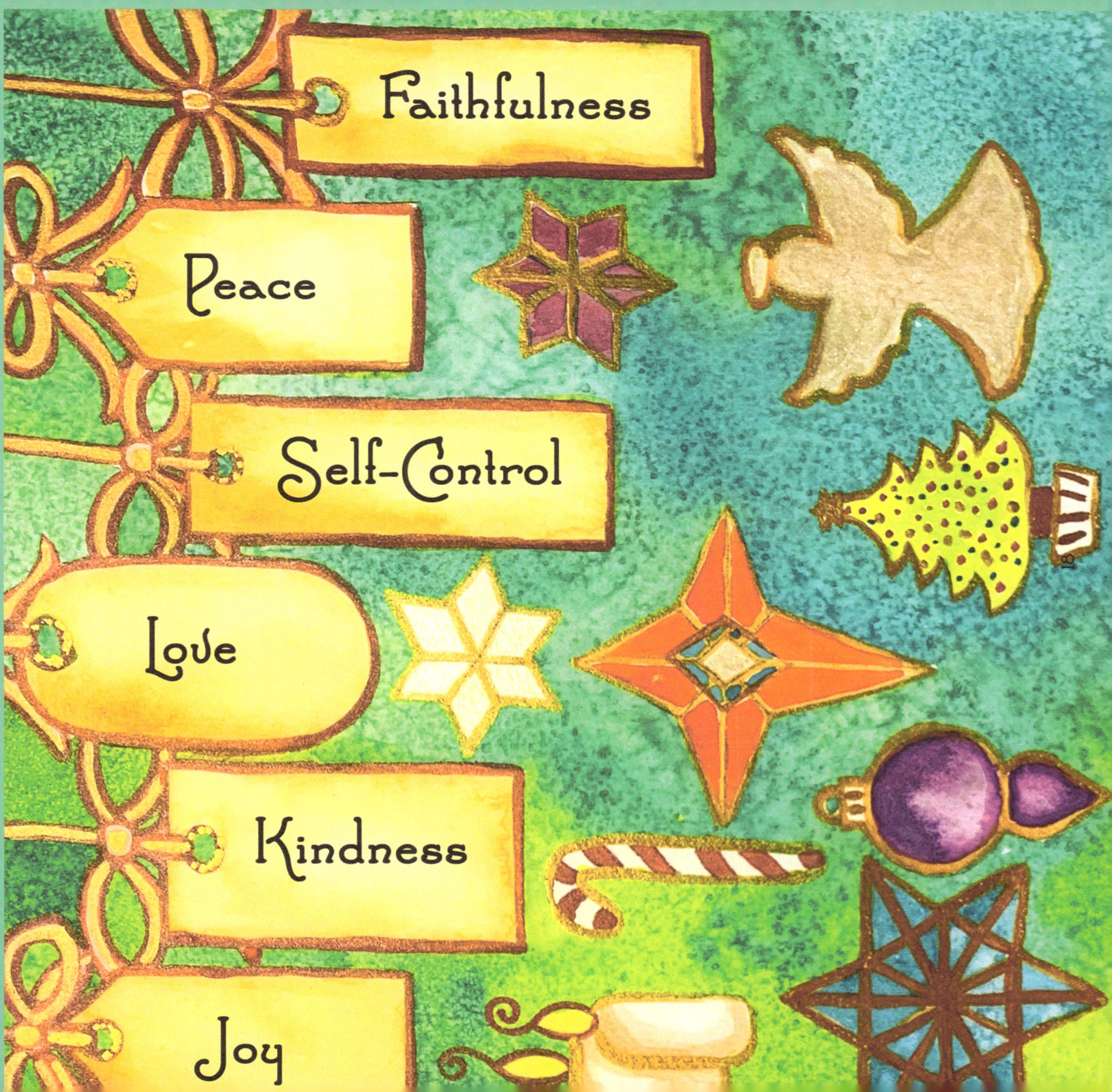

Faithfulness
Peace
Self-Control
Love
Kindness
Joy

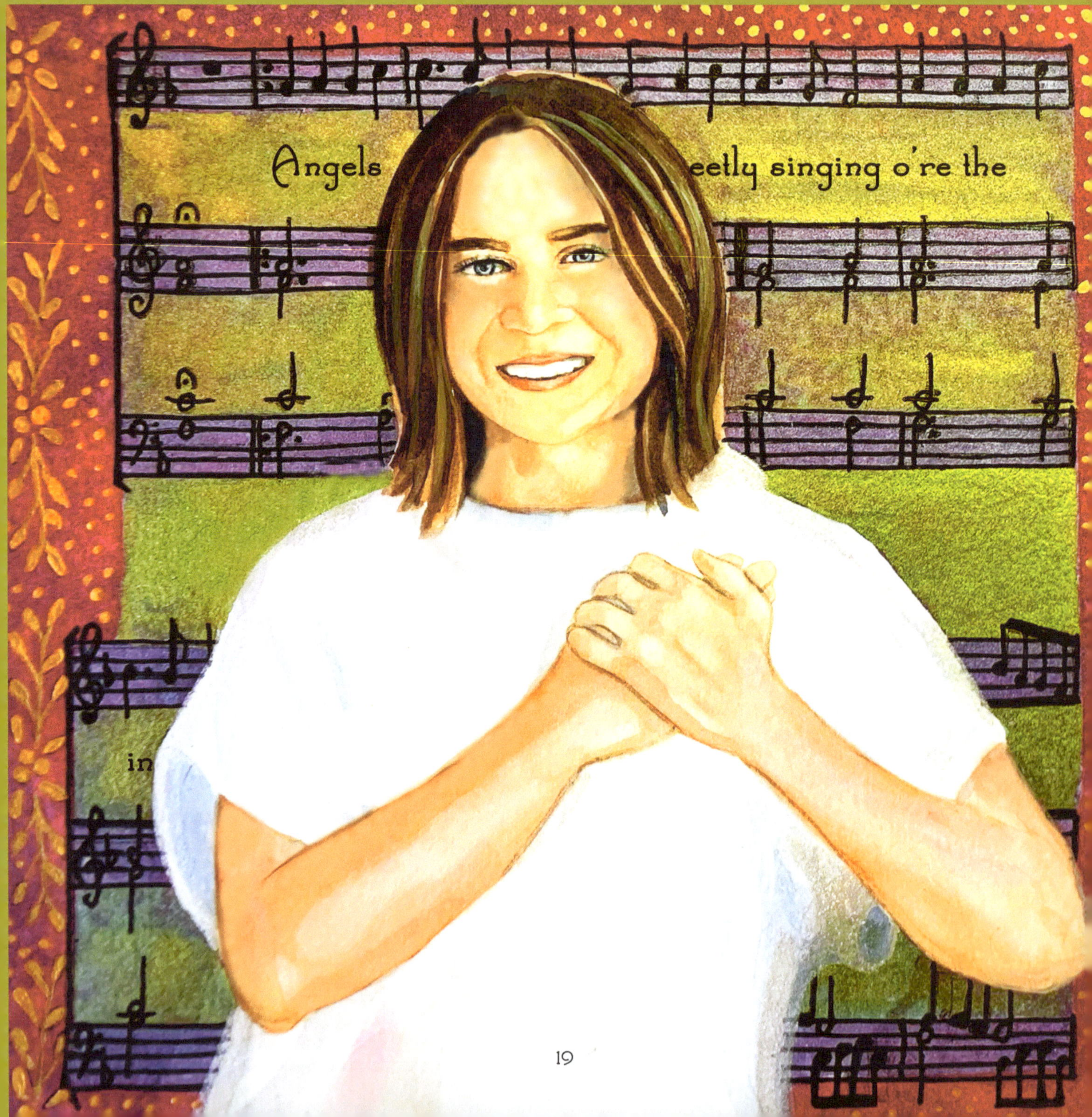
Angels ... eetly singing o're the
in

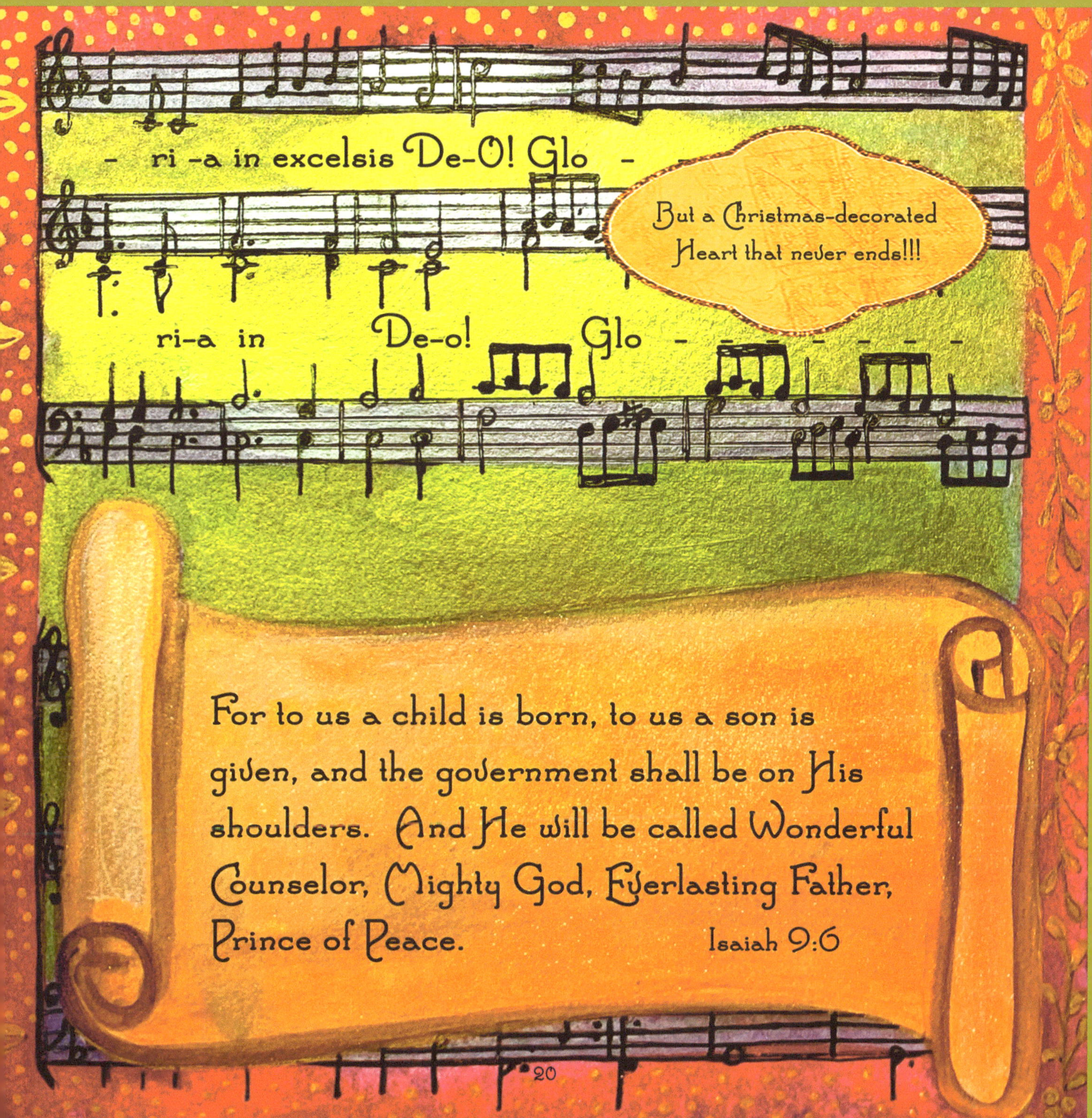
- ri -a in excelsis De-O! Glo -
ri -a in De-o! Glo -
But a Christmas-decorated Heart that never ends!!!
For to us a child is born, to us a son is given, and the government shall be on His shoulders. And He will be called Wonderful Counselor, Mighty God, Everlasting Father, Prince of Peace.
Isaiah 9:6

How I Decorated My Heart for Christmas

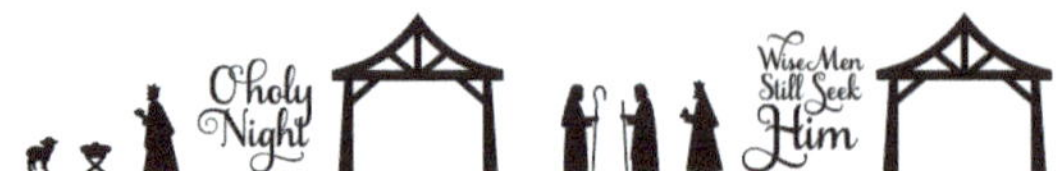

Would you like to Decorate Your Heart for Christmas?

If so begin by praying this prayer:

> Lord Jesus, I believe that you were born of the virgin Mary and came to earth to save me from my sinful life. Please forgive me of my sins and let me be born again into a new birth by the Holy Spirit. Jesus, I give my life to you, be my Lord, Saviour, Master and Friend. Thank You!!!

If you prayed this prayer Glory to God in the Highest! You can now ask God to Decorate your Heart with His wonderful gifts.

Write down what gifts He Decorated your Heart with

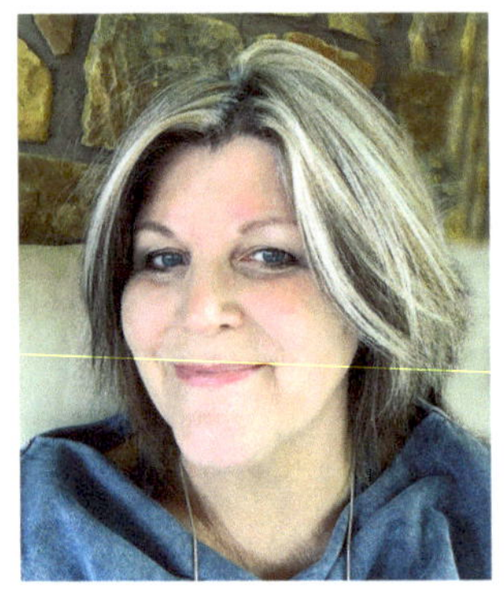 

Jan Asleson – Author/Illustrator

My designs are inspired by a desire to share with others the beauty I see
around me. My passion is to encourage others through my artistic mediums
to not give up on their dreams, to recognize the blessings all around them
and to know that there is always hope. In my life journey to know who I
am, I've discovered that what I've come to recognize as true art comes from
the greatest Artist of all, God. I believe that when we connect with each
other on a heart-to-heart level, our lives can be changed for the good.
I hope that in some way my creations will touch your heart.

I create works of beauty through mediums of paintings, metal works of
jewelry, silk art and natural textiles, portraiture, prints, books and
greeting cards.

I live in Southeast Kansas with my husband David, two horses and two
dogs. I thank God for my children and their spouses, Hannah and Scott,
Cyrus and Stephanie, and my seven grandchildren, Avery, Landen,
Brianna, Eva, Jaxson, Corbin, Xander and one on the way!

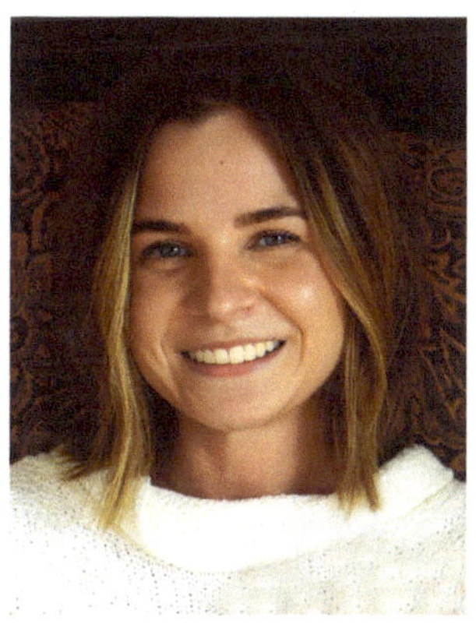

Avery Risner

Thanks to my beautiful grandaughter Avery, who was the model for this book. Avery is a graduate of MidAmerica Nazarene University with a bachelors in Organizational Leadership.

In her words - "I have had the privilage of being part of my grandmothers art work for years and it just continues to get better!' I've been so blessed to live close to family and serve my local community. I currently work at my church and help with a local nonprofit.

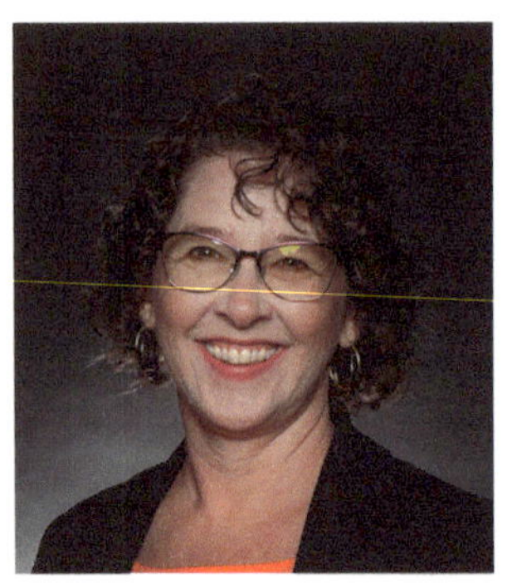

Brenda Risner

Special thanks to Brenda, my sister and friend for being my editor and for her special gift with words!

Brenda is a leader in the professional development space, she helps leaders and organizations increase productivity and organizational health by fostering healthy, people-centered cultures through communications, teamwork, and mental fitness.

Phone 816-814-4492
Email: brenda@risnerresults.com
www.risnerresults.com

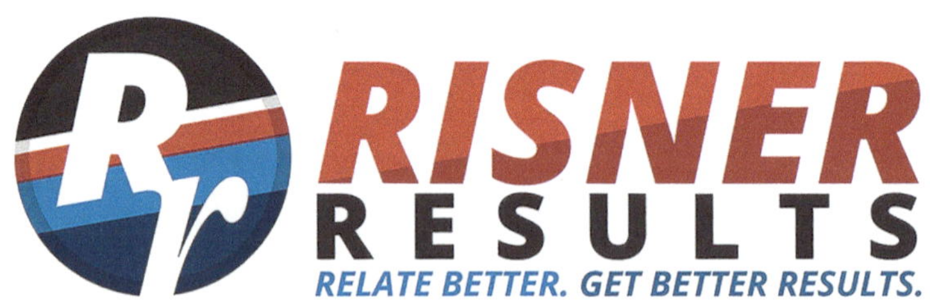

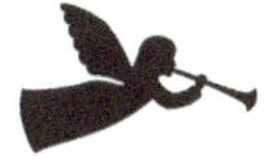

Vaneetha Risner

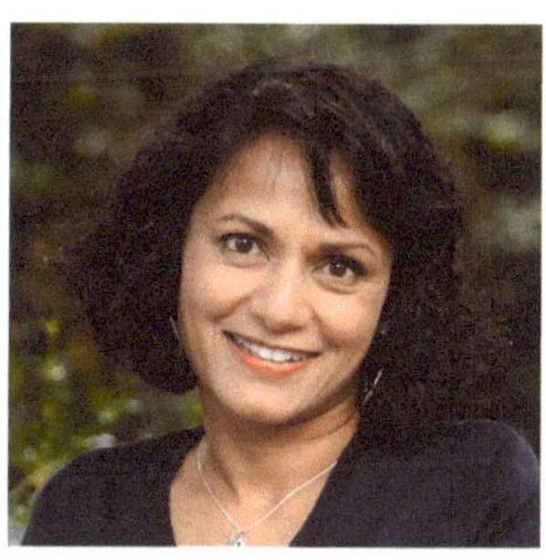

Vaneetha Risner, my sister and friend is the author of *Walking Through Fire: A Memoir of Loss and Redemption* in which she chronicles both her bewildering suffering and the breathtaking way Christ met her in it. She and her husband Joel live in Raleigh, NC where she blogs at www.vaneetha.com.

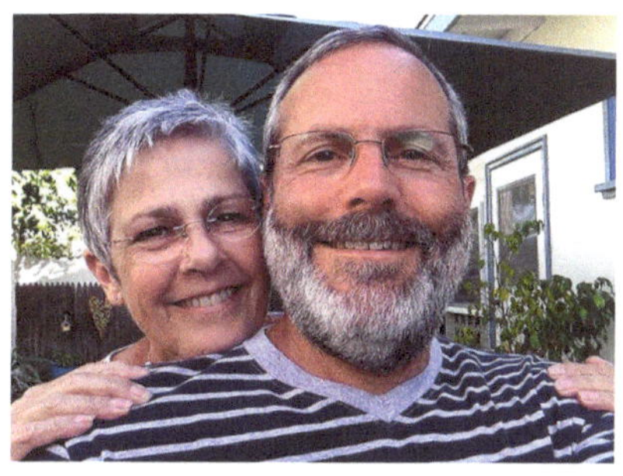

Jim Thornber

Jim Thornber is the author of *Better with Every Breath* and the pastor of Journey Church in Independence, Kansas. His previous book, *Taking Off My Comfortable Clothes*, chronicles his experience as an evangelical Protestant who was also a monk at a Catholic-based Little Portion community in Eureka Springs, Arkansas.
Connect with Jim at: www.jimthornber.com

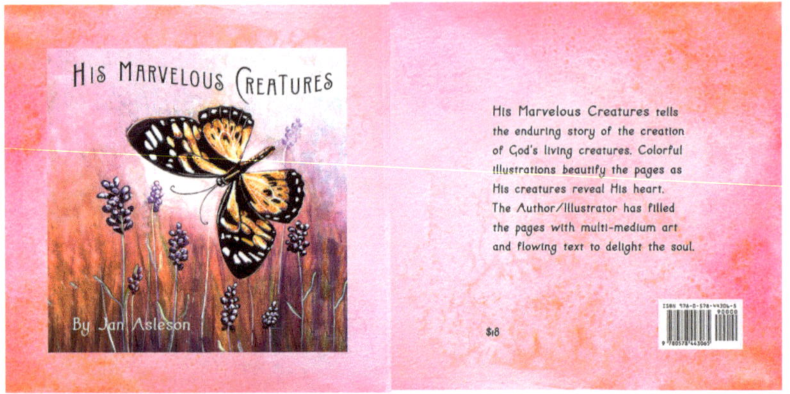

HIS MARVELOUS CREATURES
By Jan Asleson
His Marvelous Creatures tells
the enduring story of the creation
of God's living creatures. Colorful
illustrations beautify the pages as
His creatures reveal His heart.
The Author/Illustrator has filled
the pages with multi-medium art
and flowing text to delight the soul.
$18

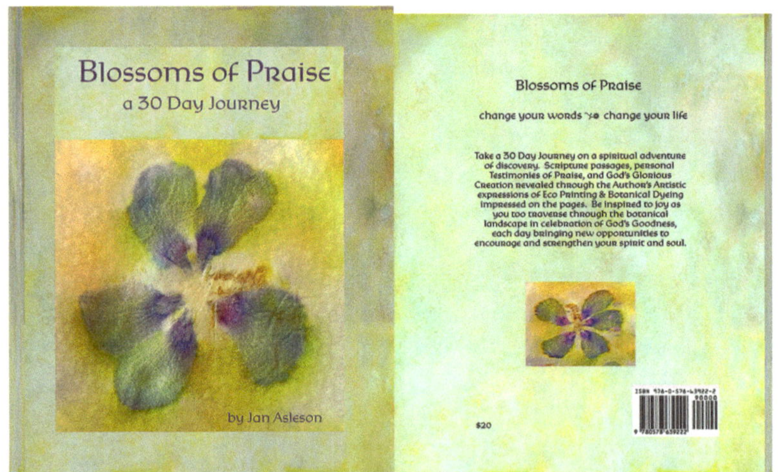

Blossoms of Praise
a 30 Day Journey
by Jan Asleson
Blossoms of Praise
change your words ~ change your life
Take a 30 Day Journey on a spiritual adventure
of discovery. Scripture passages, personal
Testimonies of Praise, and God's Glorious
Creation revealed through the Author's Artistic
expressions of Eco Painting & Botanical Dyeing
impressed on the pages. Be inspired to joy as
you too traverse through the botanical
landscape in celebration of God's Goodness,
each day bringing new opportunities to
encourage and strengthen your spirit and soul.
$20

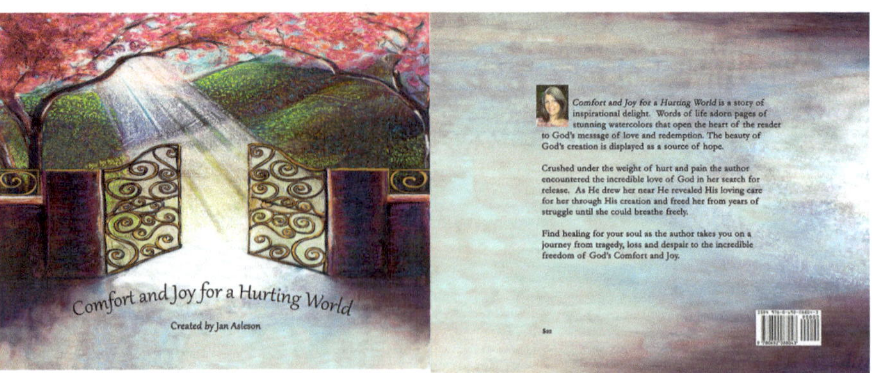

Comfort and Joy for a Hurting World
Created by Jan Asleson
Comfort and Joy for a Hurting World is a story of
inspirational delight. Words of life adorn pages of
stunning watercolors that open the heart of the reader
to God's message of love and redemption. The beauty of
God's creation is displayed as a source of hope.

Crushed under the weight of hurt and pain the author
encountered the incredible love of God in her search for
release. As He drew her near He revealed His loving care
for her through His creation and freed her from years of
struggle until she could breathe freely.

Find healing for your soul as the author takes you on a
journey from tragedy, loss and despair to the incredible
freedom of God's Comfort and Joy.